THE SERIOUS STUDENT'S PLANNER

FOR TIME MANAGEMENT SUCCESS

Activinotes

Activinotes

DAILY JOURNALS, PLANNERS, NOTEBOOKS AND OTHER BLANK BOOKS

Copyright 2016

This Book Belongs To

_____

This Week at

School...

Date:

___/___/___

Weekly Schedule for:＿＿＿＿＿＿＿＿＿＿

Subject	Monday	Tuesday	Wednesday	Thursday	Friday
Math					
Reading					
Writing					
Religion					
Social Studies					
Science					
Health					
Art					

Weekly Homework Sheet

Subject	Monday	Tuesday	Wednesday	Thursday	Friday

Daily Planner

Things to do:

Subject

Agenda:

Subject

Subject

Subject

Daily Planner

Things to do:

Subject

Subject

Agenda:

Subject

Subject

Daily Planner

Things to do:

Agenda:

Subject

Subject

Subject

Subject

Daily Planner

Things to do:

Subject

Subject

Agenda:

Subject

Subject

Daily Planner

Things to do:

Subject

Subject

Agenda:

Subject

Subject

This Week at

School...

Date:

___/___/___

Weekly Schedule for:_____

Subject	Monday	Tuesday	Wednesday	Thursday	Friday
Math					
Reading					
Writing					
Religion					
Social Studies					
Science					
Health					
Art					

Weekly Homework Sheet

Subject	Monday	Tuesday	Wednesday	Thursday	Friday

Daily Planner

Things to do:

Subject

Subject

Subject

Agenda:

Subject

Daily Planner

Things to do:

Subject

Subject

Agenda:

Subject

Subject

Daily Planner

Things to do:	Subject

Subject

Agenda: **Subject**

Subject

Daily Planner

Things to do:

Subject

Subject

Agenda:

Subject

Subject

Daily Planner

Things to do:

Subject

Subject

Subject

Subject

Agenda:

This Week at

School...

Date:

___/___/___

Weekly Schedule for:_____

Subject	Monday	Tuesday	Wednesday	Thursday	Friday
Math					
Reading					
Writing					
Religion					
Social Studies					
Science					
Health					
Art					

Weekly Homework Sheet

Subject	Monday	Tuesday	Wednesday	Thursday	Friday

Daily Planner

Things to do:	Subject

Agenda:

Subject

Subject

Subject

Daily Planner

Things to do:	Subject

Daily Planner

Things to do:

Subject

Subject

Agenda:

Subject

Subject

Daily Planner

Subject

Subject

Agenda:

Subject

Subject

Daily Planner

Things to do:

Subject

Subject

Agenda:

Subject

Subject

This Week at

School...

Date:

___/___/___

Weekly Schedule for:_____

Subject	Monday	Tuesday	Wednesday	Thursday	Friday
Math					
Reading					
Writing					
Religion					
Social Studies					
Science					
Health					
Art					

Weekly Homework Sheet

Subject	Monday	Tuesday	Wednesday	Thursday	Friday

Daily Planner

Things to do:

Subject

Subject

Agenda:

Subject

Subject

Daily Planner

Things to do:

Subject

Subject

Agenda:

Subject

Subject

Daily Planner

Things to do:

Subject

Subject

Agenda:

Subject

Subject

Daily Planner

Things to do:

Subject

Subject

Agenda:

Subject

Subject

Daily Planner

Things to do:

Subject

Subject

Agenda:

Subject

Subject

This Week at

School...

Date:

___ / ___ / ___

Weekly Schedule for:_____

Subject	Monday	Tuesday	Wednesday	Thursday	Friday
Math					
Reading					
Writing					
Religion					
Social Studies					
Science					
Health					
Art					

Weekly Homework Sheet

Subject	Monday	Tuesday	Wednesday	Thursday	Friday

Daily Planner

Things to do:

Subject

Subject

Agenda:

Subject

Subject

Daily Planner

Things to do:

Subject

Subject

Agenda:

Subject

Subject

Daily Planner

Things to do:

Agenda:

Subject

Subject

Subject

Subject

Daily Planner

Things to do:

Subject

Subject

Agenda:

Subject

Subject

Daily Planner

Things to do:

Subject

Subject

Agenda:

Subject

Subject

This Week at

School...

Date:

___/___/___

Weekly Schedule for:_____

Subject	Monday	Tuesday	Wednesday	Thursday	Friday
Math					
Reading					
Writing					
Religion					
Social Studies					
Science					
Health					
Art					

Weekly Homework Sheet

Subject	Monday	Tuesday	Wednesday	Thursday	Friday

Daily Planner

Things to do:

Subject

Subject

Agenda:

Subject

Subject

Daily Planner

Things to do:

Subject

Subject

Agenda:

Subject

Subject

Daily Planner

Things to do:

Subject

Subject

Agenda:

Subject

Subject

Daily Planner

Things to do:

Subject

Subject

Agenda:

Subject

Subject

Daily Planner

Things to do:

Subject

Subject

Subject

Agenda:

Subject

This Week at

School...

Date:

___/___/___

Weekly Schedule for:_____

Subject	Monday	Tuesday	Wednesday	Thursday	Friday
Math					
Reading					
Writing					
Religion					
Social Studies					
Science					
Health					
Art					

Weekly Homework Sheet

Subject	Monday	Tuesday	Wednesday	Thursday	Friday

Daily Planner

Things to do:

Subject

Subject

Agenda:

Subject

Subject

Daily Planner

Things to do:

Subject

Subject

Agenda:

Subject

Subject

Daily Planner

Things to do:

Subject

Subject

Agenda:

Subject

Subject

Daily Planner

Things to do:

Agenda:

Subject

Subject

Subject

Subject

Daily Planner

Things to do:

Subject

Subject

Subject

Subject

Agenda:

This Week at

School...

Date:

___/___/___

Weekly Schedule for:_____

Subject	Monday	Tuesday	Wednesday	Thursday	Friday
Math					
Reading					
Writing					
Religion					
Social Studies					
Science					
Health					
Art					

Weekly Homework Sheet

Subject	Monday	Tuesday	Wednesday	Thursday	Friday

Daily Planner

Things to do:

Subject

Subject

Agenda:

Subject

Subject

Daily Planner

Things to do:

Subject

Subject

Agenda:

Subject

Subject

Daily Planner

Things to do:

Subject

Subject

Agenda:

Subject

Subject

Daily Planner

Things to do:	Subject

Subject

Subject

Subject

Agenda:

Daily Planner

Things to do:

Subject

Subject

Agenda:

Subject

Subject

This Week at

School...

Date:

___/___/___

Weekly Schedule for:_____

Subject	Monday	Tuesday	Wednesday	Thursday	Friday
Math					
Reading					
Writing					
Religion					
Social Studies					
Science					
Health					
Art					

Weekly Homework Sheet

Subject	Monday	Tuesday	Wednesday	Thursday	Friday

Daily Planner

Things to do:

Agenda:

Subject

Subject

Subject

Subject

Daily Planner

Things to do:

Subject

Subject

Agenda:

Subject

Subject

Daily Planner

Things to do:

Subject

Subject

Agenda:

Subject

Subject

Daily Planner

Things to do:

Subject

Subject

Agenda:

Subject

Subject

Daily Planner

Things to do:

Subject

Subject

Subject

Subject

Agenda:

This Week at

School...

Date:

___/___/___

Weekly Schedule for:_____

Subject	Monday	Tuesday	Wednesday	Thursday	Friday
Math					
Reading					
Writing					
Religion					
Social Studies					
Science					
Health					
Art					

Weekly Homework Sheet

Subject	Monday	Tuesday	Wednesday	Thursday	Friday

Daily Planner

Things to do:

Subject

Subject

Agenda:

Subject

Subject

Daily Planner

Things to do:

Subject

Subject

Agenda:

Subject

Subject

Daily Planner

Things to do:

Subject

Subject

Agenda:

Subject

Subject

Daily Planner

Things to do:

Subject

Subject

Agenda:

Subject

Subject

Daily Planner

Things to do:

Subject

Subject

Agenda:

Subject

Subject

This Week at

School...

Date:

___/___/___

Weekly Schedule for:_____

Subject	Monday	Tuesday	Wednesday	Thursday	Friday
Math					
Reading					
Writing					
Religion					
Social Studies					
Science					
Health					
Art					

Weekly Homework Sheet

Subject	Monday	Tuesday	Wednesday	Thursday	Friday

Daily Planner

Subject

Subject

Subject

Subject

Daily Planner

Things to do:

Subject

Subject

Agenda:

Subject

Subject

Daily Planner

Things to do:	Subject
	Subject
Agenda:	**Subject**
	Subject

Daily Planner

Things to do:	Subject
	Subject
Agenda:	**Subject**
	Subject

Daily Planner

Things to do:

Subject

Subject

Agenda:

Subject

Subject

This Week at

School...

Date:

___/___/___

Weekly Schedule for:_____

Subject	Monday	Tuesday	Wednesday	Thursday	Friday
Math					
Reading					
Writing					
Religion					
Social Studies					
Science					
Health					
Art					

Weekly Homework Sheet

Subject	Monday	Tuesday	Wednesday	Thursday	Friday

Daily Planner

Things to do:

Subject

Subject

Agenda:

Subject

Subject

Daily Planner

Things to do:

Subject

Subject

Agenda:

Subject

Subject

Daily Planner

Things to do:

Subject

Subject

Agenda:

Subject

Subject

Daily Planner

Things to do:

Subject

Subject

Agenda:

Subject

Subject

Daily Planner

Things to do:

Subject

Subject

Agenda:

Subject

Subject

www.ingramcontent.com/pod-product-compliance
Lightning Source LLC
Chambersburg PA
CBHW081337090426
42737CB00017B/3190